To Liam X-mas '95
from Dominic Castro
& Joe

A
MAN
OF ZEN

A
MAN
OF ZEN

THE RECORDED SAYINGS
OF LAYMAN P'ANG

translated by Ruth Fuller Sasaki,
Yoshitaka Iriya, and Dana Fraser

WEATHERHILL
New York   Tokyo

First edition, 1971
Inklings edition, 1992

Published by Weatherhill, Inc., 420 Madison Avenue, 15th Floor,
New York, NY 10017. Protected by copyright under terms of the
International Copyright Union; all rights reserved. Except for fair
use in book reviews, no part of this book may be reproduced for
any reason by any means, including any method of photographic
reproduction, without permission of the publisher. Printed in the
United States.

Library of Congress Cataloging in Publication Data

P'ang, Yün, ca. 740–808.
  [P'ang chü shih yü lu. English]
  A man of Zen: recorded sayings of Layman P'ang / translated
by Ruth Fuller Sasaki and Yoshitaka Iriya. —1st ed.
      p. cm.
  Includes bibliographical references.
  ISBN 0-8348-0258-9: $7.95
  I. Zen Buddhism—Early works to 1800. I. Title.
  BQ9265.P3613 1992
  294.3'927—dc20   92-19901
                                                        CIP

Dedicated to the memory of
RUTH FULLER SASAKI
(1883–1967)

CONTENTS

ACKNOWLEDGMENTS

After the Second World War, the longtime American Buddhist and Zen student Ruth Fuller Sasaki returned to live in Kyoto in 1948 with the intention of continuing her zazen practice and traditional Rinzai Zen koan study, learning more Japanese and Chinese, and publishing scholarly English translations of important Zen texts. At her residence in Ryōsen-an, a sub-temple at Daitoku-ji, she assembled a research library and began to seek the assistance of Japanese and American scholars. Professor Yoshitaka Iriya, a specialist in T'ang and Sung colloquial Chinese, agreed to assist her work and became director of Ryōsen-an's growing research staff.

Ruth Sasaki and Professor Iriya completed a translation of the anecdotes and fifteen selected verses of Layman P'ang in late 1955. Ruth Sasaki passed away in October 1967. In 1968, I joined the research staff at Ryōsen-an. Professor Iriya and I revised the original translation of the present text. In addition, we translated ten more verses of Layman P'ang. The present English translation has been made from the Ming-dynasty woodblock edition dated 1637. Throughout the translation, our aim has been to express in English the literal meaning, style, and religious spirit of the original.

There is a great need for more English translations of complete Buddhist sutras and original Chinese Ch'an and Japanese Zen texts. The publication of *The Recorded Sayings of Layman P'ang* is a step in this direction. As it stands, it contains the work of several people. Particular mention is due Ruth Fuller Sasaki, whose breadth of vision, resourcefulness, and tireless efforts first brought the translation into being. Professor Iriya has from beginning to end been an indispensable guide in interpreting the Chinese. Gary Snyder, American poet and former Zen student at Daitoku-ji, made preliminary translations of biographies from which this translation benefited.

Special thanks are due Esei Fukutomi Oshō, priest of Ryōsen-an, for his permission to use its library; and to my teacher, Zen Master Kajitani Sōnin of Shōkoku-ji monastery, whose personal example of diligent study and living Zen spirit has encouraged me to persevere in bringing this work to completion.

Dana R. Fraser
Shōkoku-ji, Kyoto

INTRODUCTION

P'ang Yün was born in China about the year A.D. 740 and died in 808. Although he was a poor and simple man who led an ordinary life, he nevertheless attained the highest level of religious enlightenment as an ardent follower of Ch'an, that branch of Buddhism that is widely known in the West by its Japanese name of Zen. He, his wife, and their two children lived in serenity, despite the tumult of revolutions and changing times.

Layman Pang's life has inspired countless others to find for themselves the boundless Way to which he pointed in his daily life and verse. He was widely admired by the Chinese people of his day not only for the originality and vigor with which he expressed his profound religious understanding, but also for the resolve he showed in getting free of all his possessions by loading them into a boat and sinking them.

The Recorded Sayings of Layman P'ang (in Chinese, *P'ang chü-shih yü-lu*), is an account of his later years. Consisting of anecdotes about him together with his verses, it was compiled posthumously by his distinguished friend, the Prefect Yü Ti.

Famous Ch'an Buddhists appended commentaries and verses to later accounts of him. Even today, some Japanese Zen masters continue to quote him and use certain of the anecdotes as koans, or subjects for Zen meditation, for revealed in them is the timeless world of Zen, the same now as it was nearly twelve hundred years ago.

The Chinese text is valuable in its own right as one of the earliest sources of the colloquial language, and also for our understanding of Far Eastern thought.

Before describing the life of Layman P'ang, the text, and the history of this translation, a brief review of early Ch'an Buddhism may be useful for an understanding of the mid-T'ang China in which he lived.

The Rise of Ch'an Buddhism

Ch'an Buddhism may be said to have been founded by the Brahmin monk known as Bodhidharma. According to tradition he arrived in southern China by sea from India about 520. Though teachers of various types of Buddhist meditation had preceded him, none had been able to establish a school or a line of disciples. Bodhidharma did, and his successors continued the practice of seated, cross-legged meditation advocated by him and also further developed his teachings. As a reform movement, Ch'an aimed to break through the aristocratic and scholastic attitudes that characterized the established schools of Buddhism and to return to the spirit of Sakyamuni's original teaching and practice by which every person could realize Buddhahood. It held that the scriptures were but expositions in written words, and not the Buddha-mind itself. Thus, in place of the scriptural study that had occupied so much of the time of the older schools of Buddhism, Ch'an teachers gave their own discourses, and participated freely with others in lively dialogues using the everyday, colloquial language of the times. Ch'an monks rejected the subsidized life of the city temples and either returned to their earlier Buddhist practice of leading wandering and mendicant lives or, gathering around a master, settled in some remote or scarcely accessible place where master and disciples democratically lived together, cultivating the land for their daily food.

By the middle of the T'ang dynasty, Ch'an had developed into three schools, the Niu-t'ou or "Ox-head," the Northern, and the Southern. The Southern school emphasized meditation leading to the instantaneous perception of reality. Its practice was called "patriarchal" because it was held to be a continuation of the practice of the Indian founder Sakyamuni down through Bodhidharma and the succeeding Chinese patriarchs of the school. The flourishing of the Southern school during this period was due in large measure to a number of individual monks, each of whom was exceptionally capable, intelligent, and learned, and who attracted many followers.

The three distinctive teaching lines within the Southern school were the Ho-tse, the Ch'ing-yüan, and the Nan-yüeh. It was from the latter two lines that subsequently the "Five Houses" and "Seven Schools" developed through which the flower of Ch'an burst into full bloom, was transmitted to Korea, and became the Zen of Japan, which in turn became established in the West. The direct Dharma heir of Ching-yüan was Ch'an Master Shih-t'ou Hsi-chen (700–790), under whom P'ang Yün as a lay disciple first attained enlightenment. The Dharma heir of Nah-yüeh was Ch'an Master Ma-tsu Tao-i (709–88), under whom P'ang was again enlightened, and whose Dharma heir he became. Shih-t'ou and Ma-tsu were perhaps the greatest Ch'an teachers of their day. Both men were well versed in such scriptures as the Diamond Sutra, Lankavatara Sutra, Vimalakirti Sutra, and Lotus Sutra, with their doctrine that "the evil passions, as they are, are enlightenment; birth-and-death, as it is, is Nirvana," and the Nirvana Sutra, with its doctrine that "sentient beings all have the Buddha nature." They took these doctrines and expressed them in everyday terms that even unlearned country people could understand. The following statement by Kuei-feng Tsung-mi (780–841) clearly illustrates this. Tsung-mi was the fifth and last patriarch of the Hua-yen sect and also of the Ho-tse school of Ch'an. His succinct description of the Ch'an teaching of Ma-tsu and his disciples, which he terms the Hung-chou school, moreover reveals in a nutshell the significance of actions and dialogues recorded in the anecdotes of Layman P'ang. Tsung-mi said:

> The Hung-chou school asserts that our arousing
> the mind and moving thoughts, snapping the fin-
> gers, moving the eyes, etcetera, is wholly the
> activity of Buddha nature itself, and not the

movement of anything else. In a word, the entirety of our wanting something, getting angry at something, or arousing the passions—whether good or evil, pleasurable or painful—is all Buddha nature. For example, just as from wheat flour are made noodles, crackers, and various other foods, so is every single one [of these products still] the same wheat flour.

In short, there is no need to arouse the mind to stop evil thoughts, nor any need to arouse the mind to cultivate the Way. Since the Way, as it is, is mind, we cannot cultivate mind with mind; since evil is also mind, we cannot cut off mind with mind. Not trying to cut off evil or trying to cultivate good, just letting things follow their own courses and being ourselves is what they call liberation of mind. Nowhere is there either any

Dharma principle that we ought to embrace, nor any Buddha that we ought to strive to obtain. Just like the empty sky that does not increase or decrease—[so with our mind—] what need could there be to augment or amend it! And why? Because outside of our mind itself, there is absolutely not the least little thing of value to be obtained.

The Life and Character of P'ang Yün

The preface and anecdotes of *The Recorded Sayings of Layman P'ang* are the major source of the few biographical facts and dates that are known about the man. The anecdotes emphasize above all P'ang Yün's profound religious understanding. No reference is made in them to his relationship with his parents, or to the formative influences that led him early in life to become disillusioned with worldly values. Nor is there any reference to the actual wars, floods, famines, heavy taxes, and rapid inflation that occurred in China during his lifetime. How these and other historical events may have affected him we simply do not know. The following summary combines what is known and can be inferred of P'ang Yün and his family with a consideration of his poetry, his biographer Yü Ti, and the account of him recorded in the *Chodang chip*, the earliest Ch'an history. From this emerges a suggestive picture of his character and religious standpoint.

The name P'ang Yün means "Lofty Interior," and his pen name of Tao-hsuan means "Way Mystery." The date of his birth is not recorded. We may infer that it occurred around 740 from the following evidence. We are told that at the beginning of the Yüan-ho era (806–20) he returned to Hsiang province and made a home near Hsiang-yang city, his birthplace. It was there that he met Yü Ti, who was prefect of Hsiang province and who probably lived in its capital city of Hsiang-yang during the period of his administration from 798 to October 808. Yü Ti was present at the time of P'ang's death, which occurred one week after a solar eclipse. The only solar eclipse between 806 and 808 occurred on July 27, 808. This means that P'ang died on August 3 of that year, a few months before Yü Ti moved away to Ch'ang-an to take up his new post as cabinet minister. Several anecdotes of the present text refer to P'ang as being old. Since a Chinese was considered to have reached old age when he was over fifty, P'ang may well have reached an age of sixty or seventy. In this roundabout manner we may place the date of his birth as *circa* 740.

All we are told of P'ang Yün's father is that he was a Confucian, and a minor official in Hsiang-yang until he was transferred south to be prefect of the city of Heng-yang. Even this cannot be verified historically, for no record of his administration is extant. Of P'ang Yün's mother we know nothing at all. P'ang Yün accompanied his father to Heng-yang, lived in the southern part of the city, and married. He had a son and a daughter. His daughter, Ling-chao (Spirit Shining), gained a deep understanding of Ch'an. She and her father seem to have had a particularly close and affectionate relationship.

Sometime after P'ang Yün moved to Heng-yang, he built a hermitage separate from his residence and there carried on his initial religious practices. These probably included the study of Buddhist sutras and the practice of seated meditation. When he was middle-aged he gave his house away to be used for a temple, and sank his possessions and money in a nearby river in order to be rid of them forever. He apparently regarded the acquisition of wealth as an impediment to the attainment of enlightenment, and did not give it away to others for fear it would be a hindrance to them also. It is easy to imagine the wonder and surprise of his neighbors at this drastic renunciation of property. Even today his name is widely known in connection with the incident. Unfortunately, we are not told what arrangements he made for his family. In any case, we know that P'ang and his daughter subsequently earned what was probably a meager livelihood by making and selling bamboo utensils, while the one view we have of P'ang's son hoeing in the fields suggests the possibility that he supported his mother by farming.

After disposing of his possessions, perhaps in 785, he traveled to the nearby mountain of Nan-yüeh to visit the great Ch'an Master Shih-t'ou, and was at once enlightened by him. He stayed with Shih-t'ou and his disciples until 786, when he journeyed east to Kiangsi province to visit Ma-tsu. On the way, he met the man who later became the Ch'an monk named Tan-hsia T'ien-jan. T'ien-jan (Spontaneous) was an apt name for this lively person, who was to become one of P'ang's closest friends and a poet of distinction. Under Ma-tsu, P'ang experienced great enlightenment, remained afterwards for two years among the hundreds of disciples assembled there, and became a Dharma heir of that noted master.

In subsequent years Layman P'ang seems to have devoted his time between his family, presumably still in Heng-yang, and pilgrimages around central China, matching his own Ch'an understanding against all comers in the type of lively and good-humored exchanges recorded in the present text. It was during this period that he probably wrote many of the verses that have come down to us.

Layman P'ang was an amateur poet, unschooled in either the Chinese classics or conventional rules for verse composition. His favorite themes were Buddhist teaching, practice, and enlightenment on the one hand, and warnings of pitfalls on the other. At his best, he combined these subjects with vivid autobiographical images to great effect, rhyming the end-word of every other line.

Toward the end of his life, Layman P'ang wandered northward to Hsiang-yang, accompanied by his beloved daughter, Ling-chao. According to the Preface, he lived there in a rock cave twenty *li*—about seven miles—south of Lung-men shan (Deer Gate Mountain), itself twelve miles southeast of Hsiang-yang city. Layman P'ang's proximity to Hsiang-yang city gave Prefect Yü Ti the chance to visit him frequently. Until October 808, Yü Ti was both prefect of Hsiang province and the imperial commissioner of an extensive region lying on both sides of the Han River. He seems to have admired P'ang's verses, and welcomed the chance to make the poet's acquaintance.

What kind of man was Yü Ti, that he sought out and befriended Layman P'ang? He came from a distinguished family of Central Asian descent. As a prefect, he was outspoken and proud, a capable administrator, a successful and courageous military leader, and a strict authoritarian. On the other hand, he had an overbearing manner and ruled his territory like an absolute dictator. He ignored admonitions from

Emperor Te-tsung against his misdeeds, and got away with everything because the emperor was pleased with his successes. Yü Ti on his own authority even issued an order that all mendicant Buddhist monks found in his territory were to be arrested. Those caught he tried and executed. We do not know why or for how long he carried out this persecution. It ended only after Yü Ti encountered a Ch'an monk named Tsu-yü Ho-shang (731–813), who converted him. The dramatic story of their encounter as told in an early Ch'an history goes as follows:

> Tsu-yü Ho-shang was a Dharma heir of Great
> Teacher Ma-tsu, and once lived in Hsiang-yang. . .
> There was a time when Prefect Yü Ti of Hsiang-
> yang issued orders that all mendicant monks in
> his territory should be apprehended and sent [to
> the prefectural government building in Hsiang-

yang]. There was not a single monk who escaped
with his life—all were killed. . . .

Having heard the news, the Master [Tsu-yü]
wanted to visit the Prefect, so he searched among
his assembly for companions. About ten men vol-
unteered to accompany the Master. He started
out at the head of ten followers. Upon reaching
the border the ten others feared to go on. The
Master alone crossed the border. The [Prefect's]
soldiers found the Master coming, put cangues
on him, and escorted him under guard to the
capital city of Hsiang-yang. When he arrived in
front of the government building, still with
cangues on, he donned his monk's robe and
entered the courtroom.

The Prefect, seated grandly on a chair, put a
hand on the hilt of his sword and asked: "Don't

you know that the Prefect of Hsiang-yang has the freedom to put you to the sword?" The Master said: "Do you know a King of Dharma doesn't fear birth-and-death?" The Prefect said: "Ho-shang, have you ears in your head?" The Master responded: "My eyebrows and eyes are unhindered. When I, a poor monk, meet with the Prefect in an interview, what kind of hindrance could there be?"

At this the Prefect threw away his sword, donned his official uniform, bowed low, and asked: "I have heard there is a statement in the teaching that says that the black wind blows the ships, and wafts them to the land of the Rakshasas. What does this mean?" "Yü Ti!" the Master called. The Prefect's face changed color. The Master remarked: "The land of the Rakshasas is not far!" The Prefect again asked: "What about Buddha?" "Yü Ti!" the Master called again. The Prefect answered: "Yes?" The Master said: "Don't seek anywhere else." At these words the Prefect attained great enlightenment, bowed low, and became his disciple.

After this experience, Yü Ti studied Ch'an under several masters. In his subsequent support of Buddhism, he was typical of many other officials of the time. It was he who was present at the time of Layman P'ang's death and who compiled *The Recorded Sayings of Layman P'ang* as a tribute to his memory.

Layman P'ang and Ling-chao had been living in Hsiang province for about two years when the Layman made ready to die. Since no specific illness is mentioned, we may assume that in his old age he simply knew that his time had come. Here is the account from the *Chodang Chip*:

When the time came to pass on, the Layman had his daughter prepare hot water, took a bath, donned his robe, sat properly cross-legged upon his bed, and having spoken his final words addressed her, saying: "Watch when the sun reaches due south [at noon] and report it to me." As he had said, she watched and reported, saying: "The sun has just reached due south, but the sun's *yang* brilliance is eclipsed." The Layman exclaimed: "How can that be!" Then he arose and went to see it himself. Thereupon his daughter crawled upon the bed, sat properly, and passed away. Her father turned, and seeing this exclaimed: "Exquisite! I spoke of it earlier, but now I'll have to do it later." Accordingly the Layman let seven days elapse and died.

After his remains had been cremated and the ashes scattered in accordance with his last wishes, a messenger was sent to report the news to P'ang's widow, who presumably was still in Heng-yang with their son. The Preface recounts the bizarre way in which the son chose to die, and how the widow subsequently went into seclusion and disappeared. One implication of all this is that each member of the family, having attained the Way, died when the time came just as each had lived, simply and contentedly, without leaving a trace behind.

The personality of P'ang Yün defies categorization. He was true to himself and lived without attachments. He seems to have had no ambition for the Chinese ideal of an administrative career, or for political agitation or social reform. Although raised in a Confucian family, he preferred to express himself using Buddhist terms. Although described as a Buddhist lay believer, he gave away his house, destroyed his possessions, and wandered about like a monk. Even so, he also declined to become a monk, did not give lectures on Buddhism, try to train disciples, or renounce the income and possibilities for travel that his occupation of making bambooware afforded. He seems to have recommended Buddhist sutras enthusiastically in his verses because he had realized their significance in his own life, and not from any sectarian bias. He had a particular preference for the Vimalakirti Sutra, whose hero—a layman, said to have been a contemporary of Sakyamuni—had such a profound understanding of Buddhist enlightenment that he could cheerfully pursue many activities forbidden to monks without this affecting him, and moreover best all the monks in debates on Buddhist teaching.

NOTE ON THE ILLUSTRATIONS

"Ma-tsu Answering Layman P'ang" (facing p. 39), by an unknown Chinese artist of the thirteenth century; ink on silk, 105.6 x 34.8 cm.; Tennei-ji, Kyoto. Left, Layman P'ang; right, Ma-tsu answering the Layman's question.

"Layman P'ang and His Children" (facing p. 86), a woodblock frontispiece illustrating *A Hundred Dramas of the Yüan*. Shown in the courtyard of their home are, right to left, the daughter, the Layman, and the son.

"Ling-chao and Tan-hsia" (facing p. 112), a woodblock frontispiece from the same collection described above. The inscription reads: "The girl Ling-chao enlightens Master Tan-hsia."

The woodcuts sprinkled throughout the book are taken from the *Mustard Seed Garden Manual of Painting*.

THE RECORDED SAYINGS
OF LAYMAN P'ANG

compiled by
Imperial Commissioner Yü Ti

Ma-tsu answering Layman P'ang

PREFACE

The Layman, whose personal name was Yün and whose nickname was Tao-hsüan, was a native of Hsiang-yang. His father held the office of Prefect of Heng-yang. The Layman lived in the southern part of the city. There he built a hermitage, carrying on his religious practices to the west of the house, and after several years his entire household attained the Way. This was what is now Wu-k'ung Hermitage. Later he gave this former dwelling near the hermitage to be made into a temple. This was what is now Neng-jen Temple.

During the Chen-yüan era [785–804] of the T'ang dynasty, he loaded the treasure of his household—several tens of thousands of strings of cash—onto a boat in Tung-t'ing Lake to the right of the Shao

River, and sank it in the middle of the stream. After that he lived like a single leaf.

The Layman had a wife, a son, and a daughter. They sold bamboo utensils in order to obtain their morning and evening meals.

During the Chen-yüan era the Ch'an and Vinaya sects were in high favor, and the Patriarchal doctrine likewise flourished, diffusing its brilliance abroad, spreading rampant as a hop vine, and effecting its entrance everywhere. Then it was that the Layman initially visited Shih-t'ou, and in an instant his former state [of mind] melted away; later, he saw Ma-tsu and again sealed his Original Mind. [From that time on] his every act manifested his penetration of the Mystery, and there was nothing about him that did not accord with the Way. He had the boundless eloquence of Manjusri, and [everything he said] was in conformity with the Mahayana treatises on reality. After that he went about everywhere testing [men's] attainment of the Ultimate Principle.

At the beginning of the Yüan-ho era [806–20] he made his home in Hsiang-yang, living in a rock cave. (Today, the Layman's Cliff is to be seen twenty *li* to the south of Deer Gate.) At that time the Prefect Yü Ti, advancing his banners, investigated conditions by collecting the songs of the common people. He obtained the Layman's works and greatly admired him. Thereupon he took advantage of a favorable opportunity and himself visited the Layman, treating him cordially like an old and dear friend. They not only pledged their devotion, but thereafter their mutual visits continued without lapse.

When the Layman was about to die he said to his daughter Ling-chao: "Illusory transformations lack reality. I comply with whatever comes. Go out and see how high the sun is and report to me when it is noon."

Ling-chao went to the door and quickly reported: "The sun has already reached the zenith, and there's an eclipse. Do come and see it."

"Is that so," remarked the Layman.

"Yes, indeed," replied Ling-chao.

The Layman rose from his seat and looked out of the window. Thereupon Ling-chao took her father's chair and, sitting cross-legged, in an instant passed away.

The Layman turned and, smiling, said: "My daughter has anticipated me." Whereupon he gathered firewood and concluded the matter.

When seven days had passed, Mr. Yü came to inquire how he was. The Layman, putting his hand on Mr. Yü's knee, gazed at him intently for a long time, and then said: "I beg you just to regard as empty all that is existent and to beware of taking as real all that is non-existent. Fare you well in the world. All is like shadows and echoes."

As his words ended, a strange fragrance filled the room and he sat upright as if meditating. Mr. Yü hastily called to him, but he had already gone on the long journey. The wind roared over the great marsh, yet serenely carried the sound of heavenly music; the moon passed beyond Mount Sumeru, yet did not change its golden waves of color. The Layman's final request was that he be cremated and [the ashes] scattered over rivers and lakes. Thereupon the ceremonial affairs were carried out in detail, and he was cremated in the usual manner.

A messenger was then sent to report the news to

his wife. When she heard it she said: "That stupid girl and ignorant old man have gone away without telling me. How unbearable!" Then she went and spoke to her son, whom she saw hoeing in the field, saying: "Mr. P'ang and Ling-chao are both gone." Laying down his hoe, the son exclaimed "Sa!" in reply. After a time, he also died standing up. His mother said: "Stupid boy, how awfully foolish you are!" He was also cremated. Everyone marveled at this [occurrence].

Sometime afterwards Mrs. P'ang visited her friends throughout the countryside, bidding them farewell, then went into seclusion. Later, all trace of her was entirely lost. No one knew where she had gone.

The Layman often used to say:

> I've got a boy who has no bride,
> I've got a girl who has no groom;

Forming a happy family circle,
We speak about the birthless.

Besides this [verse], his profound sayings and religious verses were circulated about, but many were scattered and lost. Now for the first time they have been gathered together from the memories of men and compiled into two sections, that they may forever be available to posterity and admonish future students.

[People of] the world said: "The Layman was indeed a Vimalakirti!" How true!

He whose name is "Nameless" has written this preface. The printing blocks are stored in the Huang-po Tripitaka Pavilion.

THE ANECDOTES

The Layman P'ang Yün of Hsiang-chou, whose nickname was Tao-hsüan, was a resident of Heng-yang prefecture in Heng-chou. His family had been Confucianists for generations. While yet a youth he became aware of the defiling passions and aspired to seek the absolute truth.

Dialogues with Shih-T'ou

At the beginning of the Chen-yüan era [785–804] of the T'ang dynasty, the Layman visited Ch'an Master Shih-t'ou. He asked the Master: "Who is the man who doesn't accompany the ten thousand dharmas?"

Shih-t'ou covered the Layman's mouth with his hand. In a flash he realized!

◆

One day Shih-t'ou said to the Layman: "Since seeing me, what have your daily activities been?"

"When you ask me about my daily activities, I can't open my mouth," the Layman replied.

"Just because I know you are thus I now ask you," said Shih-t'ou.

Whereupon the Layman offered this verse:

My daily activities are not unusual,
I'm just naturally in harmony with them.
Grasping nothing, discarding nothing,
In every place, there's no hindrance, no
    conflict.
Who assigns the ranks of vermilion and
    purple?—
The hills' and mountains' last speck of dust
    is extinguished.
Supernatural power and marvelous activity—
Drawing water and carrying firewood.

Shih-t'ou gave his assent. Then he asked: "Will you put on black robes or will you continue wearing white?"

"I want to do what I like," replied the Layman. So he did not shave his head or dye his clothing.

Dialogues with Ma-tsu

Later the Layman went to Chiang-shi to visit Ch'an Master Ma-tsu. He asked Ma-tsu: "Who is the man who doesn't accompany the ten thousand dharmas?"

"Wait till you've swallowed in one swig all the water of the West River, then I'll tell you," replied Ma-tsu.

At these words the Layman suddenly understood the Mysterious Principle. He offered the verse containing the phrase, "empty-minded having passed the exam."

He remained with Ma-tsu two years, practicing and receiving instruction. He wrote a verse which says:

> I've got a boy who has no bride,
> I've got a girl who has no groom;

Forming a happy family circle,

We speak about the birthless.

◆

One day the Layman addressed Ma-tsu, saying: "A man of unobscured original nature asks you please to look upward."

Ma-tsu looked straight down.

The Layman said: "You alone play marvelously on the stringless *ch'in* [Chinese lute]."

Ma-tsu looked straight up.

The Layman bowed low. Ma-tsu returned to his quarters.

"Just now bungled it trying to be smart," then said the Layman.

◆

One day the Layman questioned Ma-tsu, saying: "What about water, which is without sinews and bones, yet can support a boat of ten thousand *hu*?"

"Here there's no water and no boat. What sinews and bones are you talking about?" replied Ma-tsu.

The hu, or Chinese bushel, was equivalent in T'ang times to about one and two-thirds U.S. bushels.

Dialogues with Yüeh-shan

The Layman went to see Ch'an Master Yüeh-shan. Yüeh-shan asked him: "Can you put this matter in the One Vehicle?"

"I do nothing each day but seek my fare," said the Layman. "How should I know if it can be put in the One Vehicle?"

"Am I right in saying you didn't see Shih-t'ou?" asked Yüeh-shan.

"Picking up one and letting one go is not the mark of a skillful fellow," returned the Layman.

"As head of the temple," said Yüeh-shan, "I have many matters to attend to."

"Take care of yourself," said the Layman and started out.

"Picking up one and letting one go is the very mark of a skillful fellow," said Yüeh-shan.

"That great question on the One Vehicle has gotten lost," said the Layman.

"Yes, yes," agreed Yüeh-shan.

The "One Vehicle" refers to the single vehicle (Ekayana), or final teaching, which leads all beings to Buddhahood, as emphasized in the Lotus Sutra.

◆

When the Layman took leave of Yüeh-shan, the Master had ten Ch'an students accompany him as far as the gate. There the Layman, pointing to the snow in the sky, said: "Lovely snow! Flake after flake does not fall another place."

"Where do they fall?" asked the Ch'an student Ch'uan.

The Layman gave him a slap.

"Don't be so crude," said Ch'uan.

"How can you call yourself a Ch'an student!" cried the Layman. "Old Yama won't let go of you."

"How about you?' returned Ch'uan.

The Layman gave him another slap and said: "Your eyes see like a blind man's; your mouth speaks like a mute's."

Yama is the lord of hell and judge of the dead.

Dialogues with Ch'i-feng

The Layman went to see Ch'i-feng. He had barely entered the temple compound when Ch'i-feng said: "What is it that this commoner keeps incessantly coming to monasteries to get?"

Looking about him on both sides, the Layman said: "Who's talking like that?" Who's talking like that?"

Ch'i-feng shouted.

"Here I am!" cried the Layman.

"Spoken straightforwardly, wasn't it?" asked Ch'i-feng.

"What's behind, eh?" asked the Layman.

Turning his head, Ch'i-feng exclaimed: "Look, look!"

"The thief in the grass met complete defeat," said

the Layman. "The thief in the grass met complete defeat."

Ch'i-feng said nothing.

◆

One day as Ch'i-feng and the Layman were walking side by side, the Layman went a step ahead, and then said: "I am better than you by one step."

"There's no back and no front," said Ch'i-feng, "yet the old gent wants to get ahead."

"The suffering of sufferings never produces such a remark," said the Layman.

"Sir, I'm afraid you won't agree," said Ch'i-feng.

"If I don't agree, what'll you be able to do?" retorted the Layman.

"If I had a stick in my hand, I'd beat you without mercy," replied Ch'i-feng.

At that the Layman gave him a punch, and then

said: "Not too good."

Ch'i-feng started to pick up a stick, but the Layman seized it. "Today this thief is completely defeated!" he cried.

"Am I clumsy, or are you skillful?" said Ch'i-feng laughing.

"We're quits, we're quits!" cried the Layman clapping his hands.

◆

One day the Layman asked Ch'i-feng: "How many *li* is it from here to the top of your peak?"

"Where have you come from?" asked Ch'i-feng.

"It's so dreadfully steep that it can't be asked about," said the Layman.

"How much [steepness] is that?" asked Ch'i-feng.

"One, two, three," said the Layman.

"Four, five, six," said Ch'i-feng.

"Why not say seven," asked the Layman.

"As soon as I said seven there would be eight," replied Ch'i-feng.

"You can stop there," said the Layman.

"You may go on," said Ch'i-feng.

The Layman shouted and went out.

Then Ch'i-feng shouted.

◆

One day the Layman said to Ch'i-feng: "One mustn't speak [of it] directly."

"Then show me Mr. P'ang's 'master' [True Self]," said Ch'i-feng.

"What's the use of being so dispirited?" asked the Layman.

"[I had] a great question, but it missed you," said Ch'i-feng.

"Just as I thought, just as I thought," returned the Layman.

Dialogues with Tan-hsia

One day Ch'an Master Tan-hsia T'ien-jan came to visit the Layman. As soon as he reached the gate he saw [the Layman's] daughter Ling-chao carrying a basket of greens.

"Is the Layman here?" asked Tan-hsia.

Ling-chao put down the basket of greens, politely folded her arms [one on top of the other] and stood still.

"Is the Layman here?" asked Tan-hsia again.

Ling-chao picked up the basket and walked away. Tan-hsia then departed.

When the Layman returned a little later, Ling-chao told him of the conversation.

"Is Tan-hsia here?" asked the Layman.

"He's gone," replied Ling-chao.

"Red earth painted with milk," remarked the Layman.

◆

Later, when Tan-hsia came to see the Layman, though the Layman saw him coming, he neither rose nor spoke to him. Tan-hsia raised his whisk; the Layman raised his mallet.

"Just this, or is there something else?" asked Tan-hsia.

"Seeing you this time is not the same as seeing you before," observed the Layman.

"Go on and belittle my reputation as you please," said Tan-hsia.

"A while ago you took a hit [from my daughter]," returned the Layman.

"If that's so," said Tan-hsia, "then you've made [my] T'ien-jan's mouth dumb."

"You're dumb because of your intrinsic nature," said the Layman, "and now you afflict me with dumbness."

Tan-hsia drew down his whisk and departed.

"Jan Acarya, Jan Acarya [Master Jan]!" called the Layman.

But Tan-hsia did not look back.

"He's come down not only with dumbness but with deafness as well," remarked the Layman.

A whisk was originally used by Indian Buddhist monks to brush away insects without injuring them. Later, the whisk was carried as a symbol of authority by Ch'an teachers. The mallet was used in Ch'an ceremonies to call the monks to order.

◆

One day Tan-hsia went again to visit the Layman. As he reached the gate they met. Tan-hsia asked: "Is the Layman here?"

"A starving man doesn't choose his food," returned the Layman.

"Is old P'ang here?" asked Tan-hsia.

"Heavens, heavens!" sighed the Layman and entered the house.

"Heavens, heavens!" sighed Tan-hsia; then [he turned and] went back.

◆

One day Tan-hsia asked the Layman: "How does today's meeting compare with yesterday's?"

"Showing me yesterday's affair just as it is, demonstrate your Ch'an eye," returned the Layman.

"As for the Ch'an eye," replied Tan-hsia, "can it put you into itself, Mr. P'ang?"

"I'm in your eye," said the Layman.

"My eye is narrow," said Tan-hsia. "Where can you find a place in it to put your body?"

"Why should this eye be narrow! Why should this body be put!" rejoined the Layman.

Tan-hsia desisted.

"If you will speak one word more," said the Layman, "this conversation can be rounded off."

Again Tan-hsia did not reply.

"As to this one word, above all others, no man can say it," remarked the Layman.

◆

One day the Layman came and stood before Tan-hsia with hands folded [on his chest]. After a little he went out. Tan-hsia paid no attention.

The Layman came back and sat down. Whereupon Tan-hsia went and stood before him with hands folded. After a little he returned to his quarters.

"I come in, you go out," said the Layman. "We aren't getting anywhere."

"This old gent comes in and goes out, comes in

and goes out—when will it end!" returned Tan-hsia.

"You haven't the slightest compassion," said the Layman.

"I have led this fellow into such a state!" exclaimed Tan-hsia.

"What have you led?" asked the Layman.

At that Tan-hsia lifted the cap from the Layman's head and said: "You're just like an old monk."

The Layman took the cap and, putting it on Tan-hsia's head, said: "You're just like a young commoner."

"Yes sir, yes, yes," assented Tan-hsia.

"You still have the old-time spirit," said the Layman.

Tan-hsia threw down the cap. "It's very much like an official's cap," he said.

"Yes sir, yes, yes," assented the Layman.

"How could I forget the old-time spirit!" said Tan-hsia.

The Layman snapped his fingers three times. "Moving heaven, moving earth," he said.

◆

One day when Tan-hsia saw the Layman coming he assumed a running attitude.

"That's the pouncing attitude," said the Layman. "Now what's the roaring attitude?"

Tan-hsia sat down.

In front of him the Layman drew the figure seven using his staff. Below it Tan-hsia drew the figure one.

"Because of the seven, the one is seen; having seen the one, the seven is forgotten," said the Layman.

Tan-hsia stood up.

"Sit a little longer," said the Layman. "There's still a second phrase coming."

"May I please put a capping-phrase to this?" asked Tan-hsia.

"Oh! Oh! Oh!" mourned the Layman and departed.

◆

When the Layman was walking with Tan-hsia one day he saw a deep pool of clear water. Pointing to it with his hand, he said: "Being as it is, we can't differentiate it."

"Of course we can't," replied Tan-hsia.

The Layman scooped up and threw two handfuls of water on Tan-hsia.

"Don't do that, don't do that!" cried Tan-hsia.

"I have to, I have to!" exclaimed the Layman.

Whereupon Tan-hsia scooped up and threw three handfuls of water on the Layman, saying: "What can you do now?"

"Nothing else," replied the Layman.

"One seldom wins by a fluke," said Tan-hsia.

"Who lost by a fluke?" returned the Layman.

◆

One day Tan-hsia dangled a rosary in his hand. The Layman came up to him and, snatching it away, said: "We two are empty-handed. It's all over now."

"Jealous old man, you can't tell good from bad," said Tan-hsia.

"I don't really get the point of your remark," said the Layman. "I won't be like this again."

"Moo, moo!" bellowed Tan-hsia.

"How fearsome you are, my teacher!" exclaimed the Layman.

"I still lack for a stick," said Tan-hsia.

"I'm old. I can't bear the stick," said the Layman.

"You callous fellow! It's no use to hit you," returned Tan-hsia.

"Still, you haven't a device to guide me," said the

Layman.

Tan-hsia gave up concerning the rosary and started out.

"You thief!" cried the Layman. "You'll never come to get it back."

Tan-hsia turned his head and laughed heartily, "Ha, ha!"

"You're defeated, thief!" cried the Layman.

Tan-hsia came up to the Layman and, grabbing him, said: "You mustn't be so reserved!"

The Layman gave him a slap.

Dialogues with Po-ling

One day when Po-ling Ho-shang and the Layman met on the road, Po-ling asked the Layman: "Have you ever shown anyone the word by which you were helped at Nan-yüeh in former days?"

"Yes, I have shown it," replied the Layman.

"To whom?" asked Po-ling.

"To Mr. P'ang," said the Layman pointing to himself.

"Certainly you are beyond the praise of even Manjusri and Subhuti," said Po-ling.

"Who is he who knows the word by which you were helped?" asked the Layman.

Po-ling put on his bamboo hat and walked off.

"A good road to you!" called the Layman.

Po-ling did not turn his head.

Manjusri is the bodhisattva representing intrinsic wisdom. Subhuti was one of the ten chief disciples of the Buddha.

◆

One day Po-ling said to the Layman: "'Whether you can speak or whether you can't, you cannot escape.' Now tell me, what is it you can't escape?"

The Layman winked.

"Outstanding!" exclaimed Po-ling.

"You mistakenly approve me," said the Layman.

"Who doesn't, who doesn't?" returned Po-ling.

"Take care of yourself," said the Layman and went off.

◆

Po-ling was sitting one day in his quarters. As the Layman entered, Po-ling grabbed him and said: "Men of today speak, men of the past spoke: what do you speak?"

The Layman gave Po-ling a slap.

"You can't speak!" cried Po-ling.

"Speak and there will be a fault," replied the Layman.

"Pay me back for the slap," demanded Po-ling.

"Try giving me a slap," said the Layman, approaching.

"Take care of yourself," said Po-ling.

◆

"As far as this eye is concerned, can it escape men's slander?" the Layman asked Po-ling one day.

"How can it escape?" replied Po-ling.

"I know well, I know well," said the Layman.

"The stick doesn't hit a man who has nothing [further] to do," said Po-ling.

"Hit me, hit me!" cried the Layman, turning his body.

As Po-ling picked up his stick and raised it, the

Layman grabbed him, saying: "Let's see you try to escape!"

Po-ling made no reply.

Dialogues with Ta-t'ung P'u-chi

The Layman had an interview one day with Ch'an Master P'u-chi. Holding up the bamboo basket in his hand, the Layman cried: "Master Ta-t'ung, Master Ta-t'ung!"

P'u-chi made no response.

When Shih-t'ou's doctrine reached you, ice melted and tiles broke," said the Layman.

"That's obvious without your mentioning it," replied P'u-chi.

Throwing down the basket, the Layman said: "Who'd have thought it isn't worth a single cash!"

"Though it isn't worth a single cash, how can one get along without it?" responded P'u-chi.

The Layman did a dance and left.

"Layman!" called P'u-chi, holding up the basket.

The Layman turned his head. P'u-chi did a dance and left.

"Returning home, returning home!" cried the Layman, clapping his hands.

◆

One day P'u-chi said to the Layman: "As for words, few men from the past to the present have been able to escape [their limitations]. As for you, can you escape them?"

"Yes sir," assented the Layman.

P'u-chi repeated the same question a second time.

"Where have you come from?" asked the Layman.

P'u-chi again repeated the same question.

"Where have you come from?" asked the Layman.

"Not only present-day men, but the men of old also had this phrase," said P'u-chi.

The Layman did a dance and went out.

"That lunatic of himself makes mistakes," remarked P'u-chi. "Who's to examine him!"

◆

One day P'u-chi visited the Layman.

"I recall that when I was in my mother's womb I had a certain word," said the Layman. "I'll show it to you, but you mustn't hold it as a principle."

"You're still separated from life," said P'u-chi.

"I just said you mustn't hold it as a principle," rejoined the Layman.

"How can I not be awed by a word that astounds people?" said P'u-chi.

"Understanding such as yours is enough to astonish people," replied the Layman.

"The very statement 'don't hold it as a principle' has become a principle," said P'u-chi.

"You're separated by not only one or two lives," said the Layman.

"It's all right for you to reprove a rice-gruel monk [like me]," returned P'u-chi.

The Layman snapped his fingers three times.

◆

The Layman went to visit P'u-chi one day. When he saw the Layman coming, P'u-chi shut the gate and said: "Wise old gentleman, don't interview me."

"Whose fault is it that you sit alone and talk to yourself?" asked the Layman.

Thereupon P'u-chi opened the gate. Just as he stepped out he was seized by the Layman, who said: "Are you wise, or am I wise?"

"Leaving aside being wise," returned P'u-chi, "how much difference is there between opening the gate and shutting the gate and revealing and concealing?"

"That very question exasperates me to death," said the Layman.

P'u-chi was silent.

"Bungled it trying to be smart," said the Layman.

Dialogue with Ch'ang-tzu

The Layman went to visit Ch'an Master Ch'ang-tzu. The Master was about to give a discourse at the time and the entire company of monks was assembled.

Stepping forward the Layman said: "Each one of you would do well to examine himself."

Ch'ang-tzu then addressed the assembly. Meanwhile the Layman stood to the right of the Master's chair.

"Without offending your 'master,' Master," said a

monk, "will you please say something?"

"Do you know Mr. P'ang?" asked Ch'ang-tzu.

"No, I don't know him," replied the monk.

"What a pity, what a pity!" cried the Layman, seizing the monk firmly.

The monk had no reply. The Layman pushed him away.

A little later Ch'ang-tzu addressed the Layman, saying: "Did that monk get a taste of the stick just now?"

"Better wait until he's willing," replied the Layman.

"You only see the sharpness of the gimlet point," said Ch'ang-tzu. "You don't see the squareness of the chisel blade."

"Such talk is all right for me," replied the Layman, "but if an outsider heard it, it wouldn't do."

"What wouldn't do?" asked Ch'ang-tzu.

"Brother, you only see the squareness of the chisel blade and don't see the sharpness of the gimlet point," replied the Layman.

Dialogues with Sung-shan

As the Layman and Sung-shan Ho-shang were drinking tea together, the Layman held up the stand of his teacup and said: "Everyone without exception is endowed with it: why can no one speak?"

"Just because everyone without exception is endowed with it, no one can speak," returned Sung-shan.

"How is it, my elder brother, that you can speak?" asked the Layman.

"I can't help but speak," replied Sung-shan.

"Obviously, obviously," returned the Layman.

Sung-shan then drank some tea.

"Elder brother, you're drinking tea. Why don't you bow to the guest?"

"To whom?" queried Sung-shan.

"To me, P'ang," replied the Layman.

"Why must I bow again?" said Sung-shan.

Later when Tan-hsia heard of this he remarked: "Had it been anyone but Sung-shan, he'd have been completely taken in by that old gent."

The Layman heard of this, and at once had a man take a message to Tan-hsia, saying: "Why not catch on before I held up the stand of my teacup?"

◆

One day as the Layman and Sung-shan were looking at a ploughing ox, the Layman pointed to the ox and said: "He is always content, but he doesn't know of *it*."

"Except for you, Mr. P'ang, who else could know his state!" said Sung-shan.

"Tell me what it is that he still doesn't know of," said the Layman.

"I haven't seen Shih-t'ou, so it's all right I can't tell you," replied Sung-shan.

"Had you seen him, what then?" asked the Layman.

Sung-shan clapped his hands three times.

◆

One day the Layman went to visit Sung-shan. Seeing the Master holding a staff, he said: "What's that in your hand?"

"I am aged. Without this I can't take a single step," replied Sung-shan.

"Be that as it may, you still retain your vigor," observed the Layman.

At that Sung-shan hit him.

"Let go the staff in your hand and let me ask you a question," said the Layman.

Sung-shan threw down the staff.

"This old fellow's earlier words don't agree with what he says later," said the Layman.

Sung-shan gave a shout.

"Within [the cry] 'Heavens!' there still is bitterness," remarked the Layman.

◆

As the Layman and Sung-shan were walking together one day they saw a group of monks picking greens.

"The yellow leaves are discarded, the green leaves are kept," said Sung-shan.

"How about not falling into green or yellow?"

asked the Layman.

"Better you tell me," said Sung-shan.

"For the two of us to be host and guest is most difficult," returned the Layman.

"Yet having come here, you strain to make yourself ruler!" said Sung-shan.

"Who doesn't!" retorted the Layman.

"True, true," agreed Sung-shan.

"To speak about 'not falling into green or yellow' is especially difficult," said the Layman.

"But you just did so," returned Sung-shan, laughing.

"Take care of yourselves," called the Layman to the group of monks.

"The monks forgive you for falling into activity," said Sung-shan.

At that the Layman went off.

◆

As Sung-shan and the Layman were talking one day, Sung-shan suddenly lifted up a ruler from the table, saying: "Do you see this?"

"I see it," replied the Layman.

"See what?" asked Sung-shan.

"Sung-shan, Sung-shan!" exclaimed the Layman.

"You mustn't say it," said Sung-shan.

"Why shouldn't I say it?" returned the Layman.

Sung-shan then threw down the ruler.

"To start and not finish infuriates me," said the Layman.

"Not so," said Sung-shan. "Today it's you who couldn't say it."

"What couldn't I say?" asked the Layman.

"To start and not finish," replied Sung-shan.

"In strength there can be weakness; in weakness

there can't be strength," said the Layman.

Sung-shan hugged the Layman. "Old boy, you didn't touch on it at all," he said.

Dialogues with Pen-hsi

What was the meaning of Tan-hsia's hitting his attendant?" the Layman asked Pen-hsi Ho-shang.

"The family elder sees people's merits and defects," replied Pen-hsi.

"Because you and I are fellow disciples, I venture to ask," said the Layman.

"If so, tell me from the beginning and I'll consult with you," replied Pen-hsi.

"The family elder shouldn't speak with you about people's rights and wrongs," said the Layman.

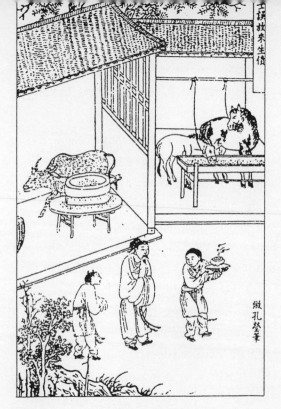

Layman P'ang and his children

"I take your age into consideration," said Pen-hsi.

"I'm sorry, I'm sorry," apologized the Layman.

◆

One day Pen-hsi saw the Layman coming. He gazed at him for quite a while. The Layman then drew a circle with his staff. Pen-hsi came forward and stepped into it.

"Thus, or not thus?" asked the Layman.

Pen-hsi then drew a circle in front of the Layman. The Layman likewise stepped into it.

"Thus, or not thus?" asked Pen-hsi.

The Layman threw down his staff and stood still.

"You came with a staff, but you go without a staff," remarked Pen-hsi.

"Luckily it's made perfect," said the Layman. "Don't trouble to watch it."

Pen-hsi clapped his hands, exclaiming: "Wonderful! There's not a thing to be attained!"

The Layman picked up his staff and, tapping the ground step by step, went off.

"Watch the road, watch the road!" called Pen-hsi.

◆

Pen-hsi asked the Layman: "What was the first word Bodhidharma spoke when he came from the West?"

"Who remembers!" said the Layman.

"You have a poor memory," said Pen-hsi.

"We mustn't speak hit-or-miss about affairs of olden days," said the Layman.

"How about affairs right now?" asked Pen-hsi.

"There's not a word to say," replied the Layman.

"To say that in front of a wise man would be still more brilliant," responded Pen-hsi.

"But you have a great eye," disagreed the Layman.

"Only when it's thus can one speak without a hint," said Pen-hsi.

"Not a single thing can be put into the eye," said the Layman.

"The sun is just at the zenith: to raise the eyes is difficult," said Pen-hsi.

"The dried skull is bored through," returned the Layman.

Snapping his fingers, Pen-hsi said: "Who could discern it!"

"What an outstanding fellow you are!" exclaimed the Layman.

Pen-hsi returned to his quarters.

Dialogue with Ta-mei

The Layman visited Ch'an Master Ta-mei. Hardly had they met when he said: "I've long wanted to meet you, Ta-mei. I wonder whether the plum is ripe or not."

"Ripe!" exclaimed Ta-mei. "What part do you want to bite?"

"Dried fruit confection," returned the Layman.

"Then give me back the pits," said Ta-mei, stretching out his hand.

The Layman went off.

Dialogues with Ta-yü

The Layman came to Ch'an Master Ta-yü's place. Ta-yü made an offering of food and presented it to the Layman. The Layman was about to accept it when Ta-yü withdrew [the food in] his hands, saying: "Long ago Vimalakirti criticized the acceptance of alms when the mind is stirred. Do you acquiesce in this action [of mine]?"

"On that occasion wasn't Subhuti an adept?" asked the Layman.

"I'm not concerned with his affair," replied Ta-yü.

"When the food reached [Subhuti's] mouth it was taken away by Vimalakirti," said the Layman.

Thereupon Ta-yü set down the food.

"There was no need for a single word," remarked the Layman.

The Vimalakirti Sutra recounts Subhuti's visit to Vimalakirti's house to beg for food. Vimalakirti filled his begging-bowl, but said that Subhuti could have it only if he regarded all food and all things in the same manner. Vimalakirti then launched into a disconcerting lecture which left Subhuti dumbfounded and wanting only to leave. Finally, Vimalakirti told Subhuti to take the food and not be upset, because all words are illusory.

◆

The Layman also asked Ta-yü: "Did Great Master Ma[-tsu] bestow on you his sincere doing for others?"

"I've not yet seen him. How should I know of his sincerity!" returned Ta-yü.

"Just such a standpoint as yours can't be sought anywhere," said the Layman.

"You mustn't keep on speaking singlemindedly," said Ta-yü.

"If I keep on speaking singlemindedly, you'll lose the principle. If I double or treble my speaking, can you open your mouth?" asked the Layman.

"This very not being able to open the mouth can be said to be true," returned Ta-yü.

The Layman clapped his hands and departed.

Dialogues with Tse-ch'uan

When the Layman met Tse-ch'uan Ho-shang, Tse-ch'uan said: "Do you still remember the doctrine of when you saw Shih-t'ou?"

"What! you mean to bring that up to me now?" rejoined the Layman.

"I am well aware that long-continued Ch'an study tends to make one slack," said Tse-ch'uan.

"You're even more decrepit that I," retorted the Layman.

"We two are contemporaries; there's little difference between us," said Tse-ch'uan.

"I'm even healthier than you," said the Layman.

"It's not that you're healthier, but that I lack your cap," observed Tse-ch'uan.

The Layman took off his cap. "Now I'm just like you," he said.

Tse-ch'uan just laughed heartily.

◆

One day as Tse-ch'uan was picking tea, the Layman said: "The Dharmadhatu doesn't contain a person. Do you see me?"

"Anyone but I would reply to your remark,"

returned Tse-ch'uan.

"Where there's a question there's an answer— that's just a commonplace," said the Layman.

Tse-ch'uan went on picking tea and paid no attention.

"Don't take offense at my casually asking a question just now," said the Layman.

Tse-ch'uan still paid no attention.

The Layman shouted, and then said: "You bad-mannered old man! Just wait till I bring this to the attention of clear-eyed men one by one!'

Tse-ch'uan discarded his tea basket and returned to his quarters.

Dharmadhatu is the unifying underlying spiritual reality regarded as the ground or cause of all things.

◆

As Tse-ch'uan was sitting in his quarters one day, the Layman saw him and said: "You only know how to sit erect in your quarters; you're not aware when a monk comes for an interview."

Tse-ch'uan dropped one leg down.

The Layman went out two or three steps, and then turned back.

Tse-ch'uan drew his leg back up.

"You're a man of complete flexibility!' the Layman exclaimed.

"But I'm the host," returned Tse-ch'uan.

"You only know there's a host, you don't know there's a guest," retorted the Layman.

Tse-ch'uan called his attendant and had him make tea.

The Layman did a dance and went out.

Dialogue with Lo-p'u

The Layman went to Ch'an Master Lo-p'u. When he had risen from saluting [Lo-p'u], he said: "In midsummer it's killing heat, in early winter freezing cold."

"Don't be mistaken," rejoined Lo-p'u.

"I'm old," said the Layman.

"Why not say 'cold' when it's cold, and 'hot'

when it's hot," said Lo-p'u.

"What's the good of catching deafness?" asked the Layman.

"I'll forgive you twenty blows," said Lo-p'u.

"You've made my mouth dumb; I've made your eyes blind," returned the Layman.

Dialogues with Shih-lin

When Shih-lin Ho-shang saw the Layman coming he raised up his whisk and said: "Without falling into Tan-hsia's [manner of] activity, try saying something."

The Layman snatched away the whisk and held up his own fist.

"That is precisely Tan-hsia's activity," said Shih-lin.

"Try not falling into it for me," said the Layman.

"Tan-hsia caught dumbness; Mr. P'ang caught deafness," rejoined Shih-lin.

"Exactly!" said the Layman.

Shih-lin said nothing.

"What I said was said casually," remarked the Layman.

◆

One day Shih-lin said to the Layman: "I have a question I'd like to ask. Don't spare your words."

"Please go on," said the Layman.

"How you do spare words!" exclaimed Shih-lin.

"Unwittingly by this discussion we've fallen into a snare [of words]," said the Layman.

Shih-lin covered his ears.

"You adept, you adept!" cried the Layman.

◆

Shih-lin was himself serving tea to the Layman one day. The Layman was about to accept tea when Shih-lin drew back and said: "How now?"

"I've a mouth but can't speak," replied the Layman.

"That's how you should be," said Shih-lin.

"How absurd!" exclaimed the Layman and, swinging his sleeves [as he turned], started out.

"Now I see through you, elder P'ang," said Shih-lin.

The Layman turned back.

"How absurd!" exclaimed Shih-lin.

The Layman said nothing.

"You should be capable of being wordless, too," remarked Shih-lin.

Dialogue with Yang-shan

When the Layman visited Ch'an Master Yang-shan, he said: "I have long wanted to meet you, Yang-shan. Now that I have arrived here, why are you facing downwards?"

Yang-shan raised up his whisk.

"Exactly!" exclaimed the Layman.

"Is this [whisk] pointing upwards or downwards?" asked Yang-shan.

The Layman struck an open-air post. "Though there's no one else [here] but us, I want to have this post testify," he said.

Throwing away his whisk, Yang-shan said: "Wherever you go, you may show this [testimony] as you please."

Dialogue with the Hermit Ku-yin

The Layman visited the hermit Ku-yin. "Who are you?" asked Ku-yin.

The Layman raised his staff.

"Isn't that the highest activity?" asked Ku-yin.

The Layman threw down his staff. Ku-yin said nothing.

"You only know the highest activity; you're unaware of the highest matter," said the Layman.

"What is the highest matter?" asked Ku-yin.

The Layman picked up his staff.

"Don't be so crude," said Ku-yin.

"What a pity you strain to make yourself ruler," returned the Layman.

"A man of uniform activity has no need to pick up a mallet or raise a whisk; nor does he use wordy replies," said Ku-yin. "If you were to meet him, what would you do?"

"Where would I meet him?" inquired the Layman.

Ku-yin grabbed hold of him.

"Is that what you'd do?" asked the Layman, and spat right into his face.

Ku-yin said nothing.

The Layman offered this verse:

> You lowered your hook into flaming water
>   where there's no fish,
> And nowhere to look for one either—I'm
>   laughing at your chagrin.
> Ku-yin, the Ch'an elder Tzu, how pitiable
>   you are;

You've been spat on, and now are ashamed
to look at me.

Layman P'ang Reads a Sutra

The Layman was once lying on his couch reading a sutra. A monk saw him and said: "Layman! You must maintain dignity when reading a sutra."

The Layman raised up one leg.

The monk had nothing to say.

The Layman Meets a Mendicant

One day the Layman was in the market place of Hung-chou selling baskets. Seeing a monk begging alms, he took out a cash and said: "Can you tell me how to appreciate alms? If you can, then I'll give you this."

The monk had nothing to say.

"You ask me," said the Layman, "and I'll tell you."

"What is it to appreciate alms?" asked the monk.

"Man seldom hears it," said the Layman. "Do you understand?" he added.

"I don't understand," said the monk.

"Who is the one who doesn't understand?" asked the Layman.

The Layman Meets a Herdboy

One day the Layman saw a herdboy. "Where does the road go?" he asked.

"I don't even know the road," replied the boy.

"You cattle-watcher!" exclaimed the Layman.

"You beast!" retorted the herdboy.

"What's the time today?" asked the Layman.

"Time for planting rice," replied the herdboy.

The Layman laughed heartily.

The Layman and the Lecture-Master

The Layman was visiting a lecture hall, listening to a discourse on the Diamond Sutra. When the "no self, no person" line was reached, he asked: "Lecture-master, since there is no self and no person, who is he who's lecturing, who is he who's listening?"

The lecture-master had no reply.

"Though I'm just a commoner," said the Layman, "I know a little about faith."

"What is your idea?" inquired the lecture-master.

The Layman replied with a verse:

> There's no self and no person,
> How then kinfolk and stranger!
> I beg you, cease going from lecture to
>   lecture;

It's better to seek truth directly.
The nature of Diamond Wisdom
Excludes even a speck of dust.
From "Thus have I heard" to "This I believe,"
All's but an array of unreal names.

When the lecture-master heard this verse, he
sighed with admiration.

Wherever the Layman dwelt there was much
coming and going of venerable priests, and many
exchanges of questions. According to the capacity of
each, the Layman responded as an echo to a sound.
He was not a man to be categorized by any rule or
measure.

*"Thus have I heard" and "This I believe" are set phrases that
mark the beginning and end of Buddhist sutras.*

Mrs. P'ang at the Temple

One day Mrs. P'ang went into the Deer Gate Temple to make an offering of food. The temple priest asked her the purpose [of the offering] in order to transfer the merit. Mrs. P'ang took her comb and stuck it in the back of her hair. "Transference of merit is completed," she said, and walked out.

It was customary for a temple priest to write on a slip of paper the donor's name, the gift and its purpose, and the date. This would then be displayed in public so that the donor's merit would become known to others, or "transferred."

The Layman and His Daughter

The Layman was sitting in his thatched cottage one day. "Difficult, difficult, difficult," he suddenly exclaimed, "[like trying] to scatter ten measures of sesame seed all over a tree!"

"Easy, easy, easy," returned Mrs. P'ang, "just like touching your feet to the ground when you get out of bed."

"Neither difficult nor easy," said Ling-chao. "On the hundred grass-tips, the Patriarchs' meaning."

◆

During the Yüan-ho era [806–20] the Layman traveled northward to Hsiang-han, stopping here and there. His daughter Ling-chao sold bamboo baskets for their morning and evening meals. The Layman had these [three] verses, which say:

When the mind's as is, circumstances also
>   are as is;
There's no real and also no unreal.
Giving no heed to existence,
And holding not to non-existence—
You're neither saint nor sage, just
An ordinary man who has settled his affairs.

Easy, so easy!
These very five skandhas make true wisdom.
The ten directions of the universe are the
>   same One Vehicle.
How can the formless Dharmakaya be two!
If you cast off the passions to enter Bodhi,
Where will any Buddha-lands be?

Ling-chao and Tan-hsia

To preserve your life you must destroy it;
Having completely destroyed it you dwell at
 ease.
When you attain the inmost meaning of this,
An iron boat floats upon water.

The five skandhas (personality aggregates) of a sentient being are: form, sensation, perception, predispositions, and consciousness. Bodhi means enlightenment.

◆

As the Layman was sitting one day he questioned Ling-chao, saying: "A man of old said: 'Bright, bright, the hundred grass-tips; bright, bright, the Patriarchs' meaning.' How do you understand this?"

"What a thing for you to say in your ripe old age," admonished Ling-chao.

"Well, what would you say?" asked the Layman.

"Bright, bright, the hundred grass-tips; bright, bright, the Patriarchs' meaning," replied Ling-chao.

The Layman laughed.

◆

The Layman was once selling bamboo baskets. Coming down off a bridge he stumbled and fell. When Ling-chao saw this she ran to her father's side and threw herself down.

"What are you doing!" cried the Layman.

"I saw Papa fall to the ground, so I'm helping," replied Ling-chao.

"Luckily no one was looking," remarked the Layman.

Layman P'ang's Death

The Layman was about to die. He spoke to Ling-chao, saying: "See how high the sun is and report to me when it's noon."

Ling-chao quickly reported: "The sun has already reached the zenith, and there's an eclipse." While the Layman went to the door to look out, Ling-chao seated herself in her father's chair and, putting her palms together reverently, passed away.

The Layman smiled and said: "My daughter has anticipated me."

He postponed [his going] for seven days.

The Prefect Yü Ti came to inquire about his illness. The Layman said to him: "I beg you just to regard as empty all that is existent and to beware of taking as real all that is non-existent. Fare you well in the world. All is like shadows and echos." His words ended. He pillowed his head on Mr. Yü's knee and died.

His final request was that he be cremated and [the ashes] scattered over rivers and lakes. Monks and laity mourned him and said that the Ch'an adherent Layman P'ang was indeed a Vimalakirti. He left three hundred poems to the world.

SELECTED VERSES

1

Of a hut in the fields the elder,
I'm the poorest man on earth!
Inside the house there's not one thing;
When I open my mouth it says "empty,
        empty."
In the past I had bad friends—
I saved them all, made them priests;
Sitting together in harmony,
I always have them hear of the Mahayana.
At mealtimes carrying bowls for them,
I serve them one and all.

2

People have a one-scroll sutra
Without form and without name.
No man is able to unroll and read it,
And none of us can hear it.
When you are able to unroll and read it,
You enter the principle and accord with the
    Birthless.
Not to speak of becoming a bodhisattva,
You don't even need to become Buddha.

3

White-robed, I don't adhere to appearances;
The true principle arises from Emptiness.
Because my mind's without obstruction
Wisdom goes forth to all directions.
I only consider the lion's roar—
I don't let wild jackals yap!
Bodhi is said to be most marvelous,
But I scold it for being a false name.

4

Traveling the path is easy,
Traveling the path is easy!
Within, without and in between I depend
     upon innate Wisdom:
Innate Wisdom being non-sentient, the
     dharmas are not born;
Birthless, I enter the true Principle.
Not form, not mind, a single radiance
     streams forth;
In the mind-ground appears the Udumbara
     tree of Emptiness.

The Udumbara tree is a legendary tree said to flower every three thousand years.

124

5

Without no other, within no self.
Not wielding spear and shield, I accord with
Buddha-wisdom.
Well-versed in the Buddha-way, I go the
non-Way.
Without abandoning my ordinary man's
affairs,
The conditioned and name-and-form all are
flowers in the sky.
Nameless and formless, I leave birth-and-
death.

"The conditioned" is that which is formed through causes and
always produces effects; also, whatever is produced continues,
changes, and is destroyed.

6

Going out of the room,

Coming into the room,

Coming and going, coming and going—
    therefore your weeping!

Coming and going was due only to greed,
    anger and folly.

Now that you've realized, you should be
    content.

Being content, you should penetrate the
    Source,

And discard your former false teachers.

Those false teachers—

Make them your handmen!

Dharma-almsgiving has no before or after;

Together you preserve the Birthless Land.

7

Without any cause you lose your mind,
And run out the front gate seeking [it].
Although you try to question old friends,
All's quiet, without any trace [of them].
But returning to the hall, when you care-
    fully consider it,
Transforming sentient beings, [in] accord
    with tranquility,
You cannot go outside and seek friends;
Of yourself, amidst your family, you enter
    Nirvana.

8

A resolute man
In the past,
But not today,
I destroyed my treasures utterly,
And ransomed back my bunch of slaves—
Six in number, male and female,
Each one having six mouths.
The double six—the thirty-six—
Always follow me fore and after.
I do not bind them, and
They do not venture to dash away.

9

If it's said that Bodhi is difficult,
Bodhi is also not difficult.
Wanting little and knowing content, the
    least is ample.
Forever free from wealth and lust, the spirit
    of itself is at ease.
I clearly perceive the Three Roads' pain,
And am not concerned with worldly fame.

The Three Roads lead to the hell of fire; the hell of blood, where beasts devour each other; and the hell of swords, where the leaves and grasses are sharp-edged swords.

10

Precisely in the middle is Mind, the King.

As is, the six roots are bright.

The six dusts are empty,

The six consciousnesses pure,

And the double six—the thirty-six—

Alike return to the Great Perfect Mirror.

11

Not old and not new,
It transforms through casual conditions into
    ten thousand million bodies.
When you have the absolute Unity,
A hundred million is like a wad of dust.

12

From the Storehouse appeared a pearl,
Gloriously brilliant and radiantly gleaming.
Who in the past fled and became a beggar—
Today returns home, a rich man's son.

13

Mind depends upon true Wisdom,
The Principle pursues activity of mind;
With Principle and Wisdom unhindered
The mind is birthless.
Deluded, there is self;
Enlightened, there is no-sentience.
With great Wisdom penetrated,
All the dharmas do not arise,
The five skandhas are masterless,
The six lands are in repose,
The seven deaths are not encountered,
The eight mirrors are completely bright,
And excellent transformations fittingly occur
In accord with the Buddha's words.

14

Reading the sutras, you must understand
    their meaning;
Understanding their meaning, you can prac-
    tice.
When you depend upon the meaning of the
    teachings
You enter the Palace of Nirvana.
When you don't understand their meaning,
With your myriad views you're worse than
    blind:
Congenial writings largely occupying your
    [mind-]ground,
The mind-ox won't consent to cultivate it;
Fields all over are covered with grass—
Where then can the rice-plants grow?

15

No-greed surpasses charity,

No-folly surpasses seated meditation,

No-anger surpasses morality,

No-thought surpasses seeking relationships.

I manifest all an ordinary man's affairs,

And at night I sleep at ease.

In winter I turn to the fireplace—

The fire that's basically smokeless.

I neither fear the demoness Blackness

Nor seek her sister Charity.

Trust in fate produces expedients;

All [ride] together in the Prajna boat.

If you understand like this,

Your merit is truly boundless.

Prajna means transcendent wisdom.

16

Not wanting to discard greed and anger,
In vain you trouble to read Buddha's
    teachings.
You see the prescription, but don't take the
    medicine—
How then can you do away with your
    illness!
Grasp emptiness, and emptiness is form;
Grasp form, and form is impermanent.
Emptiness and form are not mine—
Sitting erect, I see my native home.

Inklings Editions are a production of Weatherhill, Inc., publishers of fine books on Asia and the Pacific. Supervising editor: Margaret E. Taylor. Book design and typography: Liz Trovato. Production supervision: Bill Rose. Text composition: G & H Soho, Inc., Hoboken, New Jersey. Printing and binding: Daamen, Inc., West Rutland, Vermont. The typeface used is Berkeley Old Style.